THE
MATCHA
COOKBOOK

An Hachette UK Company
www.hachette.co.uk

First published in Great Britain in 2018 by Aster, a division of
Octopus Publishing Group Ltd, Carmelite House,
50 Victoria Embankment, London EC4Y 0DZ
www.octopusbooks.co.uk

ISBN 978-1-91202-355-4

A CIP catalogue record for this book is available from the
British Library.

Printed and bound in China.

10 9 8 7 6 5 4 3 2 1

Consultant Publisher Kate Adams
Recipe Developer and Food Stylist Nicole Pisani, Food for Happiness
Additional Recipes Oliver Pagani and Mariko Bangerter
Senior Designer Jaz Bahra
Assistant Editor Nell Warner
Copy Editor Clare Sayer
Photographer Issy Croker
Props Stylist Emily Ezekiel
Production Manager Caroline Alberti

Page 7 picture credit: Franz Eugen Köhler, Köhler's Medizinal-
Pflanzen, 1897/Wikipedia
Page 8-9 picture credit: Yanis Ourabah/Getty Images

THE
MATCHA
COOKBOOK

Discover the health benefits
and uses of matcha, with
50 delicious recipes

CONTENTS

INTRODUCTION

Matcha is a fine powder made from young green tea leaves. It comes from the tea plant *Camellia sinensis*, a shrub native to southern China. In Japanese, *cha* means 'tea' and *ma* means 'powder', so the word translates literally as powdered tea. Matcha tea is therefore different to most teas, including green, that 'steep' the leaves in hot water. With matcha tea, the whole leaf is consumed.

The first green tea seeds were brought to Japan from China, it is believed by the Zen monk Eisai, in 1191 AD. With the tea grown from these seeds, which he planted in Kyoto, Eisai introduced a new way of drinking tea, which became known as the matcha style. He also wrote the book *Kissa Yojoki* on the health benefits of tea, which promoted tea-drinking as beneficial to longevity and which popularized matcha tea in Japan at that time. Tea leaves had been eaten as a medicine before this, but it was Eisai that popularized the way of drinking matcha tea.

The early beginnings of matcha in Japan explain why it is often associated with Zen philosophy, and in particular the Japanese tea ceremony, which celebrates beauty in simplicity and ordinary things and encourages participants to bring themselves absolutely into the present moment by focusing on the drinking of tea.

Even before the tea ceremony became a popular Zen practice, monks would drink matcha before meditating as it gave them a feeling of relaxed alertness. And historically, Samurai warriors drank the tea for its energizing properties. Now, in modern-day Japan, students will often drink matcha tea before exams for that same relaxed alertness, maintaining their energy while studying and focus during the exams.

Before the 15th century, matcha tea had a very bitter taste and it was really considered more of a medicine than a drink to be savoured or enjoyed. Then, during the 15th and 16th centuries, tea growers in Japan discovered that if the tea plants were kept in the shade for 3–4 weeks before being picked in the Spring harvest, the flavour of the tea softened and became less bitter. Reducing the amount of sunlight the leaves are exposed to increases the natural amino acid and chlorophyll content in the leaves. The chlorophyll produces the vivid green colour and fresh flavour that also has a hint of umami, a slightly savoury taste often associated with Asian ingredients. After the tea plants have been kept in shade for the optimum amount of time, the leaves are hand-picked, steamed, dried and then ground by granite stone mills into the fine green powder known as matcha.

Right: Camellia sinensis
Next page: Japanese tea field plantation in Uji, Kyoto pref.

THE HEALTH BENEFITS OF MATCHA

'Tea is the ultimate mental and medical remedy and has the ability to make one's life more full and complete.'

– Myoan Eisai, *Kissa Yojoki:*
How to Stay Healthy By Drinking Tea

The positive effects felt by Zen monks and Samurai warriors many centuries ago, and so intuitively felt to be health benefits associated with drinking matcha tea, are now being supported by modern science.

All green tea is high in antioxidants due to its lack of processing; the reason matcha is considered such a powerhouse of health is because the entire leaf is consumed in the powder form, making it the most potent of all the green teas.

Matcha contains small amounts of various vitamins and minerals, but is most prized for being rich in polyphenol compounds called catechins, a type of antioxidant. Because matcha is made from ground up whole tea leaves, it is a more potent source of catechins than standard green tea, which is consumed as an infusion and so the leaves are discarded. One study found that matcha contains three times more of the catechins called epigallocatechin gallate (EGCG) – an antioxidant linked to fighting cancer, viruses and heart disease – than other standard kinds of green tea. Antioxidants are the body's defence agents and they help prevent ageing and chronic diseases. The following are all health benefits associated with matcha tea.

1. May Help Prevent Cancer

Research has shown that green tea consumption can reduce the risk of some cancers. Some of the specific cancers where risk reduction has been scientifically demonstrated include bladder cancer, breast cancer, colon cancer and prostate cancer.

2. Promotes Heart Health

Matcha tea has been shown to be the highest food level source of catechins, a group of anti-inflammatory antioxidants that help prevent heart disease. Green tea has also been shown to help lower LDL cholesterol levels, reducing the risk of stroke and hypertension.

3. High Levels of L-theanine for an Alert Calm

Matcha is said to induce a feeling of alert calm due to its mix of L-theanine and caffeine. L-theanine is an amino acid that promotes alpha waves, which lead to a state of relaxed alertness. It has been shown to benefit people diagnosed with anxiety, enhancing mood as well as aiding concentration.

4. Recovery from Exercise

Studies suggest that the catechins in matcha tea can help speed recovery in athletes whose focus is high-intensity workouts, helping to reduce muscle damage.

5. Anti-Ageing

Catechins counteract the effects of free radical from the environment, such as pollution, the sun's UV rays and chemicals, which can all cause cell damage.

THE JAPANESE TEA CEREMONY

Matcha is the tea of the beautiful and exquisite Japanese tea ceremony, which was established around the year 1570 by the Zen master Sen-no-Rikyu.

There are four principles associated with the tea ceremony:
Harmony (wa)
Respect (kei)
Purity (sei)
Tranquility (jaku)

In Japanese, the tea ceremony is called a *chado* or *sado*, meaning 'The Way of Tea'. This phrase 'The Way' is related to the Zen philosophy of always being somewhere along the way, always learning, rather than ever finished.

The tea ceremony traditionally takes place in a room that is designated just for the ceremony and is precisely four-and-a-half tatami mats in size, which is about nine square metres. The guests enter the room and the host prepares the tea with very precise, slow movements. It will be a very plain room, so that all the attention is on the tea. The room will contain a stove in the middle and a kettle hanging from the ceiling over the stove. There will be bowls to drink from, the traditional bamboo whisk, scoops and ladle, along with tea caddies. Every object in the room is symbolic. All bowls are individually made and any imperfections are actually prized, as the tea ceremony celebrates beauty in imperfection. If a bowl is broken, it might be repaired using the practice of *kintsugi*, which means 'to repair with gold'. This is where gold powder is mixed in with the repair lacquer, and so makes the repaired object even more valuable than the original.

COOKING WITH MATCHA

Vibrant green matcha lattes are probably the most well-known way of consuming matcha in the West, and now recipes are popping up everywhere on health blogs and in cooking magazines, coming up with increasingly creative ways of baking, blitzing and cooking with matcha powder. It's important to know that there are a number of different types, or 'grades' of matcha available. The two grades to look out for are 'ceremonial' grade and 'premium culinary' grade.

Ceremonial grade matcha is the highest quality green tea powder available. When drinking the classic matcha tea, it is best to use the ceremonial grade matcha powder. It is expensive but you only use a small amount to make a cup or bowl. It is a vibrant green colour and has a more delicate taste than other grades of matcha. This is because it is made from the youngest leaves, with the stems removed, and is stone-ground.

Culinary matcha powder is stronger in taste, which actually makes it better to combine with other flavours; it's also less expensive. Although it doesn't have quite the same vibrant green as ceremonial matcha, it still adds amazing colour to drinks, baked goods, dressings and sauces.

In terms of creating recipes with matcha, it is often a case of trying things out to see what works, although its slightly sweet, slightly bitter flavour goes well with dairy ingredients, citrus flavours, baked goods and dark chocolate. It also seems to add an extra layer to savoury dishes from cauliflower cheese to hummus, poached chicken and fish.

DRINKS

CLASSIC MATCHA TEA

While the traditional Japanese tea ceremony is very specific and would usually be performed by a special host, there are elements of the ceremony that are worth bringing into your own matcha tea-making. It is a ceremony of mindfulness: in the moment of tea-making all attention is on the tea, it is everything. This is a wonderful practice for being more attentive and engaged in the present, and links perfectly with the idea that matcha aids a mental state of calm alertness. While this helped the Zen monks to meditate, it can also help us to feel both relaxed and focused in our own busy lives. There is also a space for gratitude and appreciation within the ceremony, it reminds us to be thankful for and show respect to even the smallest things, such as a cup of tea.

The exact amount will vary, but try to use ceremonial grade matcha powder for making the classic tea, which is made by simply whisking with just-boiled water. Ideally your water should be 80°C rather than boiling hot, so allow it to cool a little before making your matcha tea.

1–3 small scoops of matcha powder
200–250ml just-boiled water

Add 1–3 small scoops of matcha tea to a bowl or cup, using the traditional scoop – this equates to about ¼–¾ teaspoon. You may need to experiment to find what suits your own taste.

Add a little hot water and whisk in an 'M' shape with a bamboo whisk or small whisk.

Once a paste is formed, add the remaining hot water and stir.

Enjoy each sip.

MATCHA LATTE

Our favourite way to make matcha latte is with almond or oat milk, as both
of these alternatives have a natural sweetness to complement the distinct
and slightly bitter matcha flavour.

200ml unsweetened almond or
   oat milk
½ teaspoon matcha powder
   (or to taste)
1 teaspoon honey (optional)

Heat the almond or oat milk in a small saucepan to a
gentle simmer.

In your bowl or cup, add the matcha powder and a little
of the hot milk. Whisk until you have a smooth paste.
You can then either add the remaining hot milk and froth
in the cup using a small hand-held frother, or simmer
until frothy in the saucepan and then pour gently into
your cup.

Serve with honey if you need a little sweetness.

ICED MATCHA LATTE

Watching the vibrant green colour merge with the bright white of the milk over ice makes this as beautiful a drink as it is delicious and refreshing on a summer's day.

1 teaspoon matcha powder (or to taste)
50ml just-boiled (80°C) water
1 teaspoon honey
250ml milk of choice

Add the matcha powder to a bowl along with a little of the hot water. Whisk in an 'M' shape until you have a smooth, loose paste, then mix in the remaining hot water and honey until dissolved. Leave to cool slightly.

Pour into 2 glasses filled with ice and pour over the cold milk. Stir well to serve.

ICED MATCHA TEA

This antioxidant-filled iced tea combines lime, ginger and coconut with matcha and is incredibly refreshing. Holy basil tincture is an adaptogen that basically helps the body cope more effectively with stress, but is entirely optional and caution should be taken with any natural supplements if you are pregnant or nursing.

500ml coconut water
juice of 1 lime
30g fresh root ginger, peeled
10 drops of holy basil tincture
(optional)
1 teaspoon matcha powder

In a jug, combine the coconut water and lime juice. Use a garlic press to squeeze the ginger juice directly into the jug and add the holy basil drops, if using. Stir everything together.

In a bowl, combine the matcha with a little of the coconut, lime and ginger mixture and whisk to a smooth paste. Add the loose paste to the jug and mix thoroughly.

Pour into highball tumblers filled with ice.

MATCHA LIME & LEMONADE

This isn't an everyday drink as it contains sugar, but it's perfect
for a summer weekend barbecue or picnic with friends. Feel free
to sweeten to your taste.

800ml water
60g coconut sugar or caster sugar
2 teaspoons matcha powder
100ml freshly squeezed lemon
    juice, strained
100ml freshly squeezed lime
    juice, strained
handful of mint leaves

In a saucepan, combine 200ml of the water with the
sugar and place over a low heat. Stir until the sugar
has dissolved.

Add the matcha powder to a small bowl with a little of
the hot sugar water, whisking to mix. Add this to the
remaining hot sugar water and mix well.

Pour the lemon and lime juice and remaining cold
water into a sterilized jar or bottle, then add the matcha
sugar water and give it a really good shake. Chill for at
least 30 minutes.

To serve, pour the matcha lemonade over ice and
muddle in a few fresh mint leaves with a cocktail stick.

BREAKFASTS

SODA BREAD

Soda bread is the easiest bread to bake as it requires no yeast, so all you need
to do is mix the ingredients and it's ready to go straight into the oven.
The apricots in this recipe are optional, and equally other dried fruit such
as raisins or cranberries go really well.

250g spelt flour
1 teaspoon bicarbonate of soda
2 teaspoons matcha powder
50g dried apricots, roughly
    chopped
200g natural yogurt
splash of whole milk

Pre-heat the oven to 200°C (400°F), Gas Mark 6.

Sieve the flour, bicarbonate of soda and matcha together
and stir through the apricots. Form a well in the flour
and add the yogurt, stirring as you pour. Bring the flour
and yogurt together to form a sticky dough, adding a
splash of milk if you need to.

Tip the dough onto a floured surface and knead for
just a minute to form a ball before placing on a floured
baking tray. Dust the dough ball and then score a deep
cross on the top of the ball. Bake in the oven for 45
minutes – if you tap the bottom it will sound hollow
when the loaf is baked.

SMOOTHIE BOWL

Adding a spoonful of matcha to your morning smoothie or juice is one of the easiest ways to enjoy a daily dose of antioxidants, sharpening your focus so you're ready for the day ahead. Any 'green' smoothie or juice works well with matcha, especially with ingredients like spinach, kale, cucumber, lime, avocado and pineapple.

½ avocado
½ banana, sliced and frozen
¼ cucumber, roughly chopped
25g baby spinach leaves
50ml coconut water
1 teaspoon matcha powder
squeeze of lime juice

To serve
yogurt
Matcha Granola (see page 32)

Place all the ingredients in a blender and whizz until thick and smooth. Add more or less coconut water to achieve your desired consistency.

Serve with yogurt and a sprinkling of matcha granola.

MATCHA GRANOLA

The Japanese discovered that matcha is a great ingredient for baking, adding a really interesting flavour as well as the distinctive matcha colour. As it also goes well with coconut, it makes for a really delicious nutty granola. You might also want to try making this recipe with a teaspoon of ground ginger.

250g jumbo oats
150g hazelnuts, roughly chopped
100g dried coconut flakes
50g pumpkin seeds
2 teaspoons matcha powder
2 heaped tablespoons coconut oil
60g maple syrup
1 teaspoon vanilla extract

Preheat the oven to 140°C (275°F), Gas Mark 1 and line a large baking tray with baking paper.

Mix all the dry ingredients together in a large bowl.

Heat the coconut oil and maple syrup in a small saucepan until melted and combined, then stir in the vanilla extract. Pour this into the dry ingredients and stir thoroughly so that all the oats, nuts and seeds are evenly coated.

Pour the granola into the lined baking tray and spread out evenly. Bake for about 1 hour until golden and just crunchy. Leave to cool and then gently bring up the sides of the paper to transfer the granola to an airtight jar.

MATCHA MAPLE OATS

This is such a warming way to enjoy matcha in the morning. If you soak the oats in almond milk overnight, they will be ready even faster when you heat them up for breakfast. You can use honey instead of maple syrup and add any extra toppings you like, such as sliced bananas or berries.

110g porridge oats
½ teaspoon matcha powder
200ml unsweetened almond milk
200ml water
2 tablespoons maple syrup
black (or white) sesame seeds,
   to serve

Mix the matcha into the dried oats and put into a saucepan. Add the almond milk along with the water and bring to the boil. Reduce the heat, cover and simmer for about 10 minutes, stirring every now and then.

Leave to stand for a couple of minutes with the lid on, and then pour into bowls. Drizzle over maple syrup and add some black or white sesame seeds, to serve.

PANCAKES

Delicious on a weekend morning, these pancakes puff up really well and are a great way to enjoy quinoa flour, which unlike most flours, is a good source of protein. You can use all quinoa flour in this recipe if you want to make these gluten-free.

For the pancakes

90g quinoa flour

90g spelt flour

1½ teaspoons baking powder

¼ teaspoon bicarbonate of soda

½ teaspoon sea salt

1 tablespoon matcha powder

1 egg

180g Greek yogurt, plus extra
  to serve

250ml full-fat milk (or use
  almond milk)

1 tablespoon vanilla extract

butter or coconut oil, for frying

For the bananas

2 bananas, halved lengthways

20g butter

10g coconut sugar

To serve

6 slices streaky bacon, fried

100ml maple syrup

handful of flaked almonds,
  toasted (optional)

Sift the quinoa and spelt flours into a large mixing bowl, add the rest of the dry ingredients and mix together thoroughly.

Beat the egg in a separate bowl and whisk in the yogurt, milk and vanilla extract. Add the wet ingredients to the dry and mix until combined into a thick batter.

Place a nonstick frying pan over a medium heat and add a little butter or coconut oil. Pour a small ladleful of batter into the pan once the butter or oil is melted and beginning to bubble. Cook for about 2 minutes until you see bubbles forming on the surface and then flip over, cooking the other side for about 2 minutes again.

For the bananas, heat another pan, add the butter and once it begins to bubble add the sugar. When the sugar has melted, place the banana halves in the pan and turn to coat in the sugar-butter. Cook on each side until caramelized.

Serve with maple syrup, bacon, Greek yogurt and flaked almonds.

MATCHA OMELETTE
WITH GOATS' CHEESE AND HERBS

The goats' cheese, soft egg omelette and generous handfuls of herbs in this recipe go brilliantly with matcha. This is full on and packed with protein and flavour.

4 eggs
1 tablespoon natural yogurt
1 teaspooon matcha powder
zest of ½ lime
pinch of sea salt
10g unsalted butter
1 teaspoon olive oil
50g soft goats' cheese
small handful of finely chopped
   herbs (use a mixture of basil,
   dill and chives)

Crack the eggs into a bowl and whisk with the yogurt, matcha powder, lime zest and salt.

Place a non-stick frying pan over a very high heat. When it's really hot, add the butter and oil, and when the butter starts foaming, add the egg mixture.

Let the sides fluff up, pulling the edges in with a rubber spatula to allow some of the uncooked egg to run into the spaces. Dot the goats' cheese across the omelette and scatter over the herbs.

When it is mostly cooked (the centre should still be a little runny), fold in half and slide out of the pan. Divide into two and serve immediately.

EGGY BREAD
WITH MATCHA PRAWNS

In this recipe, you make a brown matcha butter to go with the prawns and the French (or 'eggy') toast, made here with brioche. Heat the butter in the pan until it goes nutty and brown – wonderful with the lemon prawns.

20g unsalted butter, plus extra
for frying
squeeze of lemon juice
½ teaspoon chives
½ teaspoon matcha powder
1 teaspoon coconut oil
zest of 1 lemon
12 raw tiger prawns
2 eggs
dash of milk
2 slices of brioche
kombu, soaked and pea shoots,
to garnish (optional)

Melt the butter in a small saucepan, swirling it around the pan and continuing to gently cook over a low–medium heat until it starts to turn brown and smells nutty. Take off the heat and continue to swirl around as the residual heat will continue to turn all the butter brown. Add the lemon juice, and then stir in the chives and matcha.

In a large frying pan, heat the coconut oil and sauté the lemon zest over a medium heat for a minute until the aromas are released. Add the prawns and cook for just a couple of minutes, then add the matcha butter and stir through the prawns.

Meanwhile, whisk together the eggs with a dash of milk. Heat a nonstick frying pan and add a little butter. Dip the brioche slices one by one in the egg mixture and then add to the pan, cooking for about 3 minutes on each side until golden.

Serve the prawns on top of the eggy brioche and serve with sliced kombu and pea shoots, if using.

MATCHA SCRAMBLED EGGS
WITH CREAMED CORN

Matcha works brilliantly as a seasoning; here we've mixed it with some sea salt flakes. Always use a spatula when making scrambled eggs and you will have the perfect soft curds. If cream feels a little too indulgent then swap for soured cream.

For the creamed corn

25g unsalted butter

100g frozen sweetcorn, defrosted

1 teaspoon paprika

40ml single cream

For the eggs

4 eggs

10ml single cream

10g unsalted butter

To serve

¼ teaspoon matcha powder

1 teaspoon sea salt flakes

2 slices of sourdough

fresh sweet cicely leaves,
    to garnish (optional)

Place a pan over a medium heat and add the butter once hot. Once the butter is melted and beginning to bubble, add the sweetcorn and toss to coat in the butter. Add the paprika and cream and continue to toss for a few minutes until the sweetcorn is cooked through, all the flavours have combined and the cream is reduced.

For the scrambled eggs, whisk the eggs vigorously with the cream in a bowl. Heat a nonstick pan until extremely hot and add the butter. Allow to melt, then add the whisked egg mixture. Stir with a spatula to make curds until the eggs are almost done. Remove from the heat and the eggs will finish cooking in the residual heat.

Mix the matcha powder and salt together. Toast the sourdough, then add the creamed corn and scrambled eggs on top. Sprinkle with a little matcha salt and sweet cicely, if using, to serve.

SNACKS & CONDIMENTS

SHORTBREAD

Matcha and butter are a match made in heaven. The matcha adds a wonderful extra hint of flavour to these crumbly, buttery shortbread biscuits.

100g unsalted butter, softened, plus extra for greasing
50g caster sugar, plus extra for dusting
100g plain flour
50g cornflour
2 teaspoons matcha powder
pinch of sea salt

Lightly butter a baking tray.

Put the butter and sugar in a mixing bowl and use a wooden spoon or hand-held electric whisk to cream until light and fluffy.

Sift the flour and cornflour into a separate bowl and mix in the matcha power and salt until completely combined. Add this to the creamed butter and sugar and mix everything together until smooth.

Tip this mixture on to a lightly floured surface and knead to a dough. Roll out the dough to a thickness of about 1cm and use a round biscuit cutter to cut out circles, placing them on the greased tray. Chill the biscuits on the tray for 30 minutes while you preheat the oven to 180°C (350°F), Gas Mark 4.

Bake the biscuits for 20 minutes, then remove from the oven and leave for a few minutes before transferring to a wire rack and dusting with more caster sugar.

Keep in an airtight container for 3 days.

MATCHA CRANBERRY BLONDIES

Using white chocolate to make 'blondies' rather than 'brownies' not only tastes amazing, but looks amazing when combined with vibrant green matcha. For a denser texture, replace the self-raising flour with regular plain flour or spelt flour.

125g unsalted butter

300g white chocolate chips or chunks

4 eggs

250g caster sugar

230g self-raising flour

20g matcha powder

1 teaspoon sea salt

200g frozen cranberries (topping)

Preheat the oven to 180°C (350°F), Gas Mark 4 and line a 22cm square brownie tin (or similar) with baking paper.

Put the butter and half the white chocolate chips into a medium heatproof bowl and set over a pan of just simmering water, making sure that the base of the bowl doesn't touch the water. Leave the butter and chocolate to melt together while gently stirring with a rubber spatula or wooden spoon. Set aside to come to room temperature.

In a large bowl, whisk together the eggs and caster sugar for about 5 minutes, or until pale and fluffy. Add the chocolate mixture and mix until smooth. Fold in the flour, matcha powder and salt and then the remaining chocolate chips. Pour into the prepared tin, spreading the mixture evenly. Sprinkle with cranberries so they are half submerged in the batter.

Bake in the oven for 25–30 minutes, or until the top is cracked but the middle is just set. Take out of the oven and cool completely before removing from the tin and cutting into squares.

WHITE CHOCOLATE SQUARES

This is a buttery, chocolatey treat. As we've said, matcha goes well with butter, cream and chocolate, so this recipe is definitely worth making to devour on special occasions.

60ml double cream

180g white chocolate, chopped

15g salted butter

1 tablespoon matcha powder

pinch of sea salt

dried raspberries pieces,
   to garnish

Line a small 15cm baking tin with clingfilm.

Pour the cream into a saucepan and bring almost to boiling point. Remove from the heat and add the chopped chocolate, butter, matcha and salt. Stir well with a rubber spatula until completely combined.

Pour into the lined tin and use the spatula to smooth the surface. Chill in the refrigerator for 3–4 hours, or until firm. Remove from the tin by lifting up the clingfilm (or flip out on to a board). Cut into squares and sprinkle with dried raspberries pieces.

MATCHA BLISS BALLS

It's actually incredibly easy to make raw energy balls as all you have to do is just blitz everything together. This recipe is also great if you add a couple of teaspoons of raw cacao powder.

75g raw cashew nuts

30g desiccated coconut, unsweetened

120g dried apple pieces

2 teaspoons matcha powder

½ teaspoon ground ginger

2 tablespoons coconut oil

25g raw pistachio nuts, shelled and chopped, for rolling

Place all the ingredients, except the pistachios, into a food processor and blend to a paste.

Roll into balls about the size of a walnut and then roll gently in the chopped pistachios.

Chill in the refrigerator for at least 15 minutes before you enjoy.

MATCHA TEA LOAF

This is a matcha take on a traditional tea loaf, which would usually
be made with black tea. The tea is perfect for soaking the fruit so
that it is soft, making a lovely moist loaf.

350ml water

2 teaspoons matcha powder

350g mixed sultanas and raisins

butter, for greasing

2 eggs, beaten

250g self-raising flour

200g soft dark brown sugar

1 teaspoon ground ginger

Boil the water. Leave to cool for 5 minutes and then
mix a little of the hot water with the matcha powder
to form a loose paste. Add the rest of the water and
whisk until combined.

Put the dried fruit into a bowl and pour over the
matcha tea. Cover and leave to soak overnight.

Preheat the oven to 180°C (350°F), Gas Mark 4. Grease a
loaf tin with a little butter and line with baking paper.

Add the eggs, flour, sugar and ginger to the fruit
mixture and combine well. Pour the mixture into the
lined loaf tin, smoothing the surface with a spatula.
Bake for 1–1½ hours, until a skewer comes out clean
when inserted into the middle of the cake.

Turn out of the tin and cool on a wire rack. Serve sliced,
with butter if you fancy.

MAKES 8 COOKIES

◇◇◇◇◇◇

OAT AND MATCHA COOKIES

These cookies aren't quite as naughty as many other cookies but are just as nice.
If you prefer a crunchy biscuit, add a bit more flour.

1 egg, beaten

50g unsalted butter, melted
and cooled

3 tablespoons coconut sugar
or soft light brown sugar

1 tablespoon maple syrup

75g wholemeal flour

75g jumbo oats

1 teaspoon baking powder

50g dried cranberries

50g raisins

1 tablespoon matcha powder

¼ teaspoon ground ginger

Preheat the oven to 180°C (350°F), Gas Mark 4 and line
a baking tray with baking paper.

Put the egg in a bowl with the melted butter, sugar
and maple syrup. Mix all the remaining ingredients
together in a large bowl and then pour the liquid
ingredients into the dry. Mix well until combined, then
leave for 10 minutes for the ingredients to come together.

Add large spoonfuls of the mix to the lined baking tray
and push down to flatten. Bake for 15–17 minutes, or
until risen, crisp and golden at the edges (the middles
will stay quite soft).

Leave to cool on the tray for 10 minutes, then transfer
to a wire rack to cool completely. Keep in an airtight
container for up to 3 days.

CHEESE AND MATCHA SCONES

These cheesy scones are the perfect showcase for a spot of matcha-inspired baking.

450g self-raising flour, plus extra
for dusting
1 teaspoon sea salt
1 tablespoon matcha powder
100g chilled unsalted butter, cut
into small cubes
250g mature Cheddar cheese,
finely grated
120ml cold milk or buttermilk
120ml cold water
1 egg, beaten with a splash of milk

Preheat the oven to 220°C (425°F), Gas Mark 7.

Put the flour, salt and matcha powder into a large bowl and mix together until well combined. Add the butter and rub it into the flour with your fingertips until it looks grainy.

Add 225g of the cheese and then stir to combine. Mix in the milk and water, until the dough just comes away from the edge of the bowl. Transfer to a lightly floured surface and flatten the dough into a rough rectangle about 2.5 cm thick. Using a sharp knife, cut into 6 large triangles. Gently push any offcuts together to cut more shapes.

Put the unbaked scones on a baking tray lined with baking paper and brush with the egg and milk mixture. Sprinkle the remaining cheese over the tops and bake for about 12 minutes, or until golden. Transfer to a wire rack to cool before serving.

SOUPS & SIDES

MATCHA SALT

Matcha works well when you think of it as a seasoning, adding just that last hint or layer of flavour as a finishing touch to a dish. This matcha salt is delicious with eggs (see page 41), and to season fish or meat.

---

1 tablespoon sea salt flakes

½ teaspoon matcha powder

Combine the salt and matcha. Voila.

LEMON MATCHA BUTTER

Having a flavoured butter on hand means that you can add amazing flavour to the simplest of dishes. This lemon matcha butter is particularly good with any pan-fried or baked fish, from lemon sole to cod (or anything that looks good that day at the fishmonger). Cook your fish as normal and add a disc of flavoured butter at the end, allowing it to melt in the pan and spooning the melted butter over the fish as it rests.

125g butter

zest of 1 lemon

1 tablespoon matcha powder

Allow the butter to become soft enough so that you can beat in the lemon zest and matcha.

Shape into a log and chill it, then once cold, wrap the log in clingfilm, knotting the ends, so that you can unwrap and slice off discs of butter.

MATCHA PICKLES

Pickling and fermenting have come back into fashion, especially as these methods of preserving food are also very healthy. You'll need sterilized jars for these recipes: just pour just-boiled water over your clean jars, empty out the water and leave them to air-dry. Pickles are a really good way to add a burst of flavour to a simple dish, such as a sandwich, spring rolls (see page 94), fish or a burger (see page 102).

For the pickled eggs

6 eggs

250ml cider vinegar

150ml water

50g coconut sugar

1 teaspoon sea salt

1 teaspoon fennel seeds

1 teaspoon mustards seeds

3 bay leaves

1 whole green chilli

1 tablespoon matcha powder

For the pickled vegetables

1 large carrot, cut into batons

1 large cucumber, cut into batons
  (remove the watery middles)

½ medium cauliflower, cut into
  small florets

¼ onion, sliced

250ml brown rice vinegar

150ml water

50g coconut sugar

1 teaspoon sea salt

1 teaspoon matcha powder

For the pickled eggs, bring a pan of water to the boil. Add the eggs and boil for 6 minutes, then run under cold water before peeling and placing in a sterilized jar. Meanwhile, put all the remaining ingredients into a pan, bring to the boil and simmer for a couple of minutes.

Allow the pickling liquor to cool a little and then pour over the eggs. Seal and when cool, transfer to the refrigerator, where they will keep for up to 4 weeks.

For the pickled vegetables, prepare the vegetables and put into a sterilized jar. Make the pickling liquor as above and pour over.

MATCHA AND RED LENTIL HUMMUS

Hummus is such a great healthy snack; here we've used lentils instead of chickpeas, although you can easily swap them. If using chickpeas, it's a good idea to add a little water and olive oil to the mix.

100g dried red lentils, rinsed and drained
1 garlic clove, crushed
juice of ½ lemon, or to taste
1 tablespoon tahini
¼ teaspoon sea salt
¼ teaspoon matcha powder

Add the red lentils to a saucepan, along with enough water to cover by a centimetre.

Bring to the boil, then reduce the heat and simmer for about 15 minutes, or until cooked and soft. Drain and set aside to cool.

Add the cooled lentils to a food processor or blender along with the remaining ingredients and blend to a soft, hummus-like consistency.

Taste and adjust the seasoning, adding more lemon juice if needed.

MATCHA BUCKWHEAT BROTH

Buckwheat is an ancient grain-like seed that is a great gluten-free alternative to wheat. It also comes in noodle form, which would work equally well in this recipe.

600ml chicken or vegetable stock
1 lemongrass stalk, bashed
100g buckwheat
1 tablespoon coconut oil
100g cavolo nero or kale, stalks
    removed and leaves shredded
1 teaspoon grated fresh root
    ginger
½ teaspoon matcha powder
2 tablespoons wheat-free tamari
    soy sauce

Bring the stock to the boil in a saucepan. Add the lemongrass and buckwheat, reduce to a simmer and cook for about 10 minutes, or until the buckwheat is tender.

Meanwhile, heat the coconut oil in a frying pan or wok, add the greens, ginger and matcha powder and sauté for about 5 minutes, adding the soy sauce just as the greens become tender.

Remove the lemongrass and divide the broth between two bowls, topping with the ginger matcha greens.

SPICED WATERCRESS AND MATCHA SOUP

The intense, vibrant green of this soup sings its own healthy praises,
plus it has flavour to match.

---

1 tablespoon olive oil
1 leek, sliced
2 teaspoons matcha powder
pinch of cayenne pepper
¼ teaspoon ground ginger
⅛ teaspoon ground cloves
¼ teaspoon ground coriander
¼ teaspoon ground cardamom
½ teaspoon grated nutmeg
350g spinach
150g watercress, plus extra to
    garnish
½ teaspoon sea salt
good pinch of black pepper
600ml hot vegetable stock
handful of hazelnuts, chopped
    (optional)

Heat the olive oil in a saucepan and add the leek. Sauté over a medium heat for 10 minutes until soft. Add the matcha powder and all the ground spices, stirring and cooking for another 5 minutes.

Add the spinach, watercress, salt and pepper and stir through, then add the hot stock and stir just until the leaves have wilted. Use a hand-held blender to blitz as soon as possible, to retain the bright green colour. Garnish with extra watercress and a sprinkling of chopped hazelnuts, if liked.

RAMEN

You can take any of the elements in this dish and combine them however you like,
adding different vegetables or proteins that you fancy, such as pork, chicken or tofu.
Matcha noodles are great if you can find them, or just use your favourite noodles.

100g matcha noodles (or any soba
    noodles)
2 eggs
350ml chicken or vegetable stock
1 teaspoon matcha powder
1 teaspoon green curry paste
4 dried or fresh kaffir lime leaves
1 tablespoon fish sauce
250ml water
100g raw king prawns
200g flaked poached salmon
50g mangetout, sliced in half
1 spring onion, sliced
50g beansprouts
anise hyssop leaves or any fresh
    herb, to serve

Cook the noodles in boiling water following the
instructions on the packet. Refresh in cold water
and drain.

Meanwhile, bring a saucepan of water to the boil, add
the eggs and boil for 6 minutes (or longer if you prefer
hard-boiled). Cool under running cold water before
peeling and slicing into halves. Set aside.

Put the stock into a large pan and stir in the matcha
powder, curry paste, lime leaves, fish sauce and water.
Bring to a simmer and cook for 15 minutes to infuse
the flavours. Add the raw prawns and leave to simmer
for another 5 minutes until they turn pink. Remove from
the heat and add the flaked salmon.

Divide the noodles between 2 deep bowls and pour
over the broth, dividing the prawns and salmon
evenly between the two. Garnish with the egg halves,
mangetout, spring onion, beansprouts and herb leaves,
if using.

COURGETTE FRITTERS

Feta and courgette have long been a successful pairing, and go really well here with the distinct flavour of matcha. This is another great recipe for when you have friends over to share a few dishes together around the table.

2 courgettes, grated
1 large egg
50g feta cheese, crumbled
10g dill, finely chopped
½ teaspoon sea salt
1 teaspoon matcha powder
100g plain flour (or use gluten-free gram flour)
400ml vegetable oil
mixed baby leaf salad, to serve
Matcha Lime Yogurt (see page 114), to serve

Line a colander with a muslin cloth and add the grated courgettes. Leave to drain overnight (or for speed you can squeeze the grated courgette in the muslin after 10 minutes).

Beat the egg in a large bowl and then add the crumbled feta and chopped dill. Squeeze the courgettes one more time and add to the mix, along with the salt, and mix thoroughly with a fork.

Mix the matcha powder and flour together and then add to the bowl. Use your hands to mix all the ingredients together until well combined.

Pour the oil into a large frying pan, preferably cast-iron or nonstick, and place over a medium-high heat until shimmering. With 2 hot spoons, shape one third of the fritter mix into 2 equally-sized quenelles and lower into the oil. Let the fritters cook undisturbed until browned on the underside, about 2–3 minutes. Turn over gently with tongs and cook until browned on the other side, another 2–3 minutes.

Remove the fritters from the pan and place on a large plate lined with kitchen paper; repeat with the remaining mixture to make 6 fritters in total.

Transfer to a serving plate and serve warm, at room temperature or cold with baby leaf salad and some Matcha Lime Yogurt for dipping.

WHITE ASPARAGUS
WITH MATCHA VINAIGRETTE
AND QUAIL EGGS

White asparagus is only in season for a short time, but is absolutely delicious if you come across it. It's thicker than green asparagus, but is usually very tender and sweet.

½ garlic clove, finely grated
1 teaspoon Dijon mustard
½ teaspoon honey
2 tablespoons white wine vinegar
1 teaspoon matcha powder
3 tablespoons olive oil
8 quail eggs
8–12 white asparagus spears
(or use 16–20 green asparagus spears)
4 teaspoons ground flaxseed (optional)
sea salt and ground black pepper

Mix together the garlic, mustard, honey, vinegar and matcha powder. Add the oil gradually, whisking hard so you end up with a creamy vinaigrette.

Bring a saucepan of water to the boil. Lower the quail eggs in and cook for 2½ minutes. Remove from the water and place straight into a bowl of cold water before peeling.

Snap off and discard the tough ends of the asparagus and then shave the spears using a peeler so you end up with very thin slices of asparagus – don't worry about making them overly neat. Divide the asparagus shavings between each plate so it covers the whole plate.

Cut the quail eggs in half and lay 4 halves randomly on each plate. Spoon over the creamy matcha vinaigrette and dust with ground flaxseed, if using. Season with salt and pepper and serve.

MATCHA MISO AUBERGINE

Sweet miso aubergine is so easy and so delicious. Matcha makes a good addition to the classic recipe as it goes well with ginger and soy. Here we've used furikake to scatter over the roasted aubergines – it's a brilliant Japanese seasoning made from black and white sesame seeds and seaweed flakes. It's available in Asian supermarkets and a number of high-street supermarkets and health food stores, but if you can't find it then sesame seeds work perfectly here, too.

2 aubergines

1 heaped tablespoon white miso paste

1 tablespoon honey

1 tablespoon soy sauce

1 teaspoon toasted sesame oil

1 teaspoon grated fresh root ginger

1 teaspoon matcha powder

3 spring onions, shredded

2 teaspoons furikake (or sesame seeds)

Preheat the oven to 180°C (350°F), Gas Mark 4.

Slice the aubergines in half lengthways and score the flesh in a diamond pattern. Place the aubergine halves, scored side up, on a baking tray.

Mix the miso, honey, soy sauce, sesame oil, ginger and matcha powder together, adding just a little water to loosen to a smooth paste. Brush this over the aubergines.

Roast in the oven for about 20 minutes, or until golden in colour and soft all the way through. Serve scattered with the shredded spring onion and sprinkle over the furikake (or sesame seeds).

BAKED MATCHA CAULIFLOWER

You can make this vegan by leaving out the Cheddar at the end, although it does add wonderful colour and a bit of extra lusciousness. The white miso, while optional, will add a boost of umami flavour.

1 medium whole cauliflower

1½ tablespoons coconut oil

1 onion, quartered

2 garlic cloves, halved

400ml oat milk

2 teaspoons matcha powder

225g cashew nuts (soaked overnight or for at least 4 hours)

50g brewer's yeast or nutritional yeast

1 teaspoon white miso (optional)

generous handful of grated mild Cheddar cheese (optional)

sea salt and ground black pepper

red sorrel, to garnish (optional)

Preheat the oven to 220°C (425°F), Gas Mark 7.

Remove the largest outer leaves from the cauliflower and discard, then cut the cauliflower into quarters. Bring a deep saucepan of salted water to the boil. Boil the cauliflower for 10 minutes until tender and then remove and place on a baking tray.

Meanwhile, melt the coconut oil in a saucepan, and fry the onion and garlic over a medium heat until slightly transparent, then add the oat milk and matcha powder and bring to the boil. Once boiled, pour this mixture into a blender and add the drained cashew nuts, yeast and white miso, if using. Blend on a high speed for 2 minutes until you have a very smooth luxurious sauce. Season to taste and add the sliced cauliflower leaves.

Pour this béchamel all over the cauliflower. Sprinkle the Cheddar over the top and then roast in the oven for 20 minutes. Garnish with red sorrel, if using.

SOURED CUCUMBER SALAD
WITH GOATS' CURD

This is delicious as part of a summer barbecue or gathering. You can make a big batch of the cucumbers as they'll keep for up to a month: just double or triple the quantities.

For the cucumbers
200ml white wine vinegar
2 tablespoons caster sugar
1 teaspoon pink peppercorns
1 tablespoon mustard seeds
2 baby cucumbers, chopped into
    wedges
1 teaspoon sea salt
50g dill
120ml goats' curd

To serve
4 slices wholemeal bread, toasted
½ teaspoon Matcha Salt (see
    page 58)
20g dill

Heat the vinegar, sugar, peppercorns and mustard seeds in a saucepan, stirring until the sugar has dissolved. Leave to cool.

Place the cucumber wedges in a colander and toss with the salt. Leave to stand for 15 minutes before transferring to a sterilized jar (see page 61) along with the dill. Pour over the cooled vinegar and sugar solution and seal with an airtight lid. The cucumbers will be sour enough to eat a day later, but will keep up to a month in the refrigerator, becoming more sour over time.

Spread the curd on a serving plate and arrange the cucumber wedges on top. Serve with toast and finish by sprinkling over the Matcha Salt, dill and a little pickling liquor.

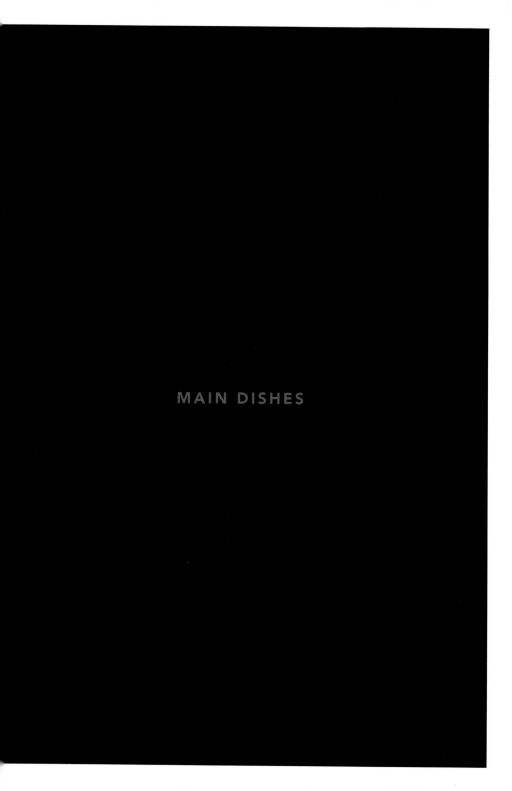

MAIN DISHES

BACON, LETTUCE AND MATCHA SALAD

This salad is really quick and you could also include chicken or swap the bacon for tofu for a vegetarian option. The Matcha Lime Yogurt is versatile and goes very well with this salad as a dressing.

1 teaspoon unsalted butter

4 slices of streaky bacon, cut into 2.5cm slices

100g Matcha Lime Yogurt (see page 114)

1 teaspoon ume shiso seasoning or cider vinegar

2 baby gem lettuces, leaves separated

1 ripe avocado, peeled, stoned and cut into small pieces

3 hard-boiled eggs, halved

For the matcha crisps

1 potato

2 tablespoons olive oil

1 teaspoon Matcha Salt (see page 58)

To serve

Parmesan shavings

a handful of pea shoots

2 spring onions, sliced

First make the matcha crisps. Preheat the oven to 120°C (250°F), Gas Mark ½.

Slice the potato as thinly as possible with a mandolin or sharp knife. Pat dry with kitchen paper and then toss in the olive oil and Matcha Salt. Tip on to a baking tray and bake for 2 hours, turning over halfway through, until golden. Remove from the oven and rest for 10 minutes to continue crisping up.

In the meantime, heat a frying pan and cook the bacon in the butter until crispy.

Combine the Matcha Lime Yogurt with the ume shiso seasoning or vinegar to loosen. Put the lettuce leaves into a large mixing bowl and gently combine with the yogurt dressing until evenly coated. Place in a serving dish, then add the avocado, bacon, egg and matcha crisps.

To serve, sprinkle over the Parmesan, pea shoots and spring onions.

MATCHA MUSHROOM SPELT RISOTTO

Mushrooms go really well with matcha, especially when helped along with a little butter, as in this recipe. Shiitake and shimejii mushrooms are used here but this risotto would work equally well with chestnut mushrooms.

160g spelt grains, soaked overnight, rinsed and drained
1 tablespoon olive oil
1 small onion, finely chopped
300ml hot vegetable or chicken stock
1 tablespoon unsalted butter
100g mixed shimejii and shiitake mushrooms, cleaned
½ teaspoon matcha powder
1 tablespoon yeast flakes or grated Parmesan cheese
sea salt
red lace mustard leaves, to garnish (optional)

Add the spelt grains to a saucepan and cover well with water. Bring to the boil, then simmer for 20 minutes. Drain, rinse and set aside the grains.

Sauté the onion in the olive oil in a large saucepan over a medium heat for about 10 minutes, then add the grains, stirring to coat all the grains in the oil.

Ladle half the hot stock into the grains, bring to the boil, then reduce to a gentle simmer and cook for about 10 minutes, stirring occasionally. Add more stock as needed to cook the spelt and create a risotto-like texture.

Meanwhile, melt the butter in a separate pan and sauté the mushrooms and matcha powder with a little sea salt.

Either stir the mushrooms through the cooked spelt or pile the mushrooms on top of the spelt in bowls. Sprinkle with yeast flakes or grated Parmesan and garnish with red lace mustard leaves, if using.

MATCHA NOODLES
WITH TOFU

Like matcha, ingredients such as kombu seaweed and furikake, which is a Japanese seasoning made with sesame needs and nori (seaweed) flakes, are more easily available to buy in supermarkets, Asian stores or online. For a simpler version of the broth, you can use miso instead of the kombu and lemongrass and add the matcha, mirin and tamari as below.

400ml vegetable stock
1 sheet of kombu
1 lemongrass stalk, bashed
4–6 dried shiitake mushrooms
2 teaspoons matcha powder
1 tablespoon mirin
2 tablespoons tamari
200g matcha noodles
200g firm tofu, cut into cubes
2 teaspoons nori flakes
1 teaspoon sesame seeds
1 tablespoon sesame oil
1 pak choi, roughly chopped
squeeze of lime juice
baby salad leaves, to garnish
 (optional)

To make the dashi broth, put the kombu into a saucepan with the hot vegetable stock, lemongrass, shiitake mushrooms and matcha powder. Bring to the boil and simmer for 20 minutes. Remove and discard the kombu and lemongrass and add the mirin and tamari.

Bring a large saucepan of water to the boil, add the noodles and simmer for about 6 minutes, or according to the instructions on the packet, until cooked. Drain, and then refresh with cold water before adding to the broth.

Put the tofu into a bowl, sprinkle over the nori flakes and sesame seeds and toss the tofu cubes so that they are evenly coated.

Heat the sesame oil in a pan and sauté the pak choi over a medium heat for a couple of minutes.

To assemble, divide the broth and noodles between bowls and top with the tofu and pak choi. Squeeze over the lime juice and serve with baby salad leaves, if using.

TROUT
WITH MATCHA PISTACHIO CRUMB

Matcha goes brilliantly with lots of nuts, including hazelnut, almond and
pistachio nuts, used here. With this pistachio crumb the colours combine to create
a vibrant green crunch that is perfect for fish. If trout isn't in season, this crumb is
also delicious with salmon, cod or hake.

25g raw unsalted pistachios
1 teaspoon matcha powder
1 tablespoon breadcrumbs
1 tablespoon olive oil
zest of 1 lime (then cut the zested
   lime into slices)
1 large or 2 small whole rainbow
   trout, gutted and cleaned (ask
   your fishmonger)
small handful of soft herbs, such
   as parsley, chives or coriander
sea salt and ground black pepper

To serve (optional)
75g mixed salad leaves
100g heritage tomatoes, thickly
   sliced
extra virgin olive oil

Preheat the oven to 200°C (400°F), Gas Mark 6 and line
a baking tray with baking paper.

Put the pistachios, matcha powder and breadcrumbs
into a food processor and blitz for about 10 seconds until
the pistachios are a crumb-like texture, but not too fine.
Mix with the olive oil and lime zest.

Put the trout on the lined baking tray. With a sharp
knife make 3 diagonal slits along the top of the fish.
Season generously and stuff the cavity or cavities with
any herbs you wish plus the lime slices.

Press the matcha pistachio crumb all over the top of
the trout, reserving some for the tomato salad. Bake in
the oven for 8–10 minutes until the fish is opaque in
the middle.

Serve with a tomato salad, if liked. Arrange the baby
salad leaves and sliced tomatoes in a bowl, scatter over
some of the pistachio crumb and drizzle with extra
virgin olive oil.

SOLE
WITH MATCHA BEURRE BLANC AND GREENS

This matcha beurre blanc is the perfect way to marry matcha with any white-fleshed fish, such as Dover or lemon sole but you could use cod, sea bass or any sustainable white fish.

1 tablespoon vegetable oil

1 Dover or lemon Sole, skinned and trimmed but kept whole

100g curly kale, thickly sliced

100g cavolo nero, thickly sliced

For the matcha beurre blanc

½ garlic clove, sliced

1 shallot, thinly sliced

1 lemongrass stalk, crushed

2.5cm fresh root ginger, peeled and sliced

200ml white wine

60ml white wine vinegar

1 teaspoon matcha powder

350g chilled butter, diced

squeeze of lemon juice

sea salt

For the matcha beurre blanc, put the garlic, shallot, lemongrass, ginger, wine, vinegar and matcha into a saucepan and bring to the boil. Simmer until the liquid has reduced down by two-thirds.

Remove the lemongrass and reduce the heat to low, then add the chilled butter to the liquid one piece at a time, each time making sure the butter has been fully incorporated into the liquid before adding the next. Strain out the remaining ingredients and you should be left with a thickened, glossy liquid. Add a squeeze of lemon juice and season to taste. Keep the sauce somewhere warm to stop the butter solidifying.

Heat the vegetable oil in a large frying pan over a medium heat. When hot, place the sole, top down, into the frying pan. Leave for 3–4 minutes, depending on size, until golden, then turn over and cook for another 2–3 minutes.

While the sole is cooking, steam the greens until just cooked, about 3–4 minutes.

Make a bed of the greens on a large plate and place the sole in the middle. Coat the sole in the beurre blanc, making sure the greens get a liberal coating too.

SALMON
WITH ALMOND BUTTER MATCHA CRUMB

This is a brilliant way to dress up a simple weekday supper. Like nuts, seeds take
on the flavour of matcha really well, along with the mustard and lime.

2 thick salmon fillets, about 130g
each

3 teaspoons wholegrain mustard

2 tablespoons coarse almond
butter

30g pumpkin seeds, lightly
crushed

zest of 1 lime

²⁄₃ teaspoon matcha powder

1 teaspoon olive oil

1 teaspoon honey

1 tablespoon vegetable oil

sea salt and ground black pepper

lime juice, to serve

Preheat the oven to 240°C (475°F), Gas Mark 9.

Season both sides of the salmon fillets with a light
sprinkling of sea salt and leave to one side.

In the meantime, put 1 teaspoon of the wholegrain
mustard into a bowl with the almond butter, pumpkin
seeds, lime zest, matcha, olive oil and honey and mix
thoroughly to make the crumb. Season with light pinch
of salt and a heavier amount of pepper.

Pat the salmon fillets dry and then spread the flesh side
with the remaining mustard. Evenly spread the crumb
on top.

Heat the vegetable oil in an ovenproof frying pan over a
medium-high heat. Add the salmon fillet, skin side down,
pressing them down lightly until they have relaxed and
stopped tensing. Transfer to the oven and cook for 4–5
minutes until the green of the crumb is slightly browned
and the salmon fillets are medium-rare.

Squeeze lime juice over the salmon before serving.

SUMMER ROLLS
WITH MATCHA DIPPING SAUCE

Summer rolls, also called 'fresh spring rolls', are a traditional Vietnamese dish made with rice wrappers, raw vegetables and aromatic leaves. The filling often contains prawns, too, although here we've used lightly steamed fish. Using lettuce or a leaf to line the wrapper before adding your filling adds a delicious extra layer; we've used anise hyssop but iceberg lettuce works really well, too. In this recipe matcha features both in the pickled vegetables and the dipping sauce.

8 rice paper wrappers
large handful of anise hyssop
    leaves (or use 4 iceberg lettuce
    leaves, halved)
80g Matcha Pickled Vegetables
    (see page 60)
200g steamed salmon or sea bass,
    flaked
40g baby leaf spinach
40g coriander leaves

For the dipping sauce
1 tablespoon coconut sugar
2 tablespoons lime juice
1 tablespoon fish sauce
½ teaspoon matcha powder
1 garlic clove, crushed
1 green chilli, thinly sliced
1 spring onion, thinly sliced

Fill a large bowl with warm water. Working in batches, soak 2 rice paper wrappers in water until softened, about 2 minutes. Remove the wrappers from the water and arrange in single layer on your work surface.

Place a few anise hyssop leaves or an iceberg leaf in the centre of each wrapper. Place a few strips of pickled vegetables in the centre, then a spoonful of steamed fish then another few strips of the pickled vegetables. Add a drizzle of the pickling liquid for flavour and a few baby spinach and coriander leaves.

Fold one edge of each wrapper over the filling. Fold in the ends and then roll up the rice paper wrappers tightly, enclosing the filling. Transfer to a serving plate and repeat with remaining wrappers and filling.

To make the dipping sauce, whisk the sugar, lime juice and fish sauce together until dissolved, then whisk in the matcha powder before adding all the other ingredients. Serve in a bowl alongside the summer rolls.

MATCHA POACHED CHICKEN

The lemongrass in this recipe goes very well with matcha, while poaching the chicken makes it very tender. If you want to be even healthier, replace the new potatoes with another green vegetable.

10g unsalted butter

2 teaspoons matcha powder

1 tablespoon nori flakes

2 stalks of lemongrass, bashed

400ml chicken stock

4 chicken thighs

100g new potatoes, washed and halved if large

10g Lemon Matcha Butter (see page 58)

200g asparagus, woody ends snapped off

100g baby leeks

Melt the unsalted butter in a heavy-based saucepan over a medium heat and stir in the matcha powder, nori flakes and lemongrass. Pour in the chicken stock and bring to the boil.

Add the chicken breasts, reduce to a simmer and poach for about 15 minutes. Remove the chicken from the poaching liquid and leave to rest. Return the pan to the heat and increase to high to reduce the poaching liquid by half.

Meanwhile, cook the new potatoes in a separate saucepan until tender when pierced with a knife, then drain.

Melt the Lemon Matcha Butter in a frying pan over a medium heat and add the asparagus and baby leeks. Sauté until tender, about 8 minutes. Remove the vegetables and then place the poached chicken thighs skin side down in the hot pan to crisp the skin.

Serve the chicken with the potatoes, asparagus and the reduced poaching liquid drizzled over.

PORK LOIN
WITH CELERIAC MATCHA
PUREE, FENNEL AND HAZELNUT

This recipe is very versatile as the celeriac matcha purée also goes
really well with chicken. The fennel salad adds the perfect element
of crunch and freshness.

400g pork loin

100g hazelnuts

1 fennel bulb

2 tablespoons sherry vinegar

2 tablespoons extra virgin olive oil

large handful of chopped parsley

1 teaspoon vegetable oil

sea salt and ground black pepper

a handful of watercress, to garnish

For the celeriac matcha purée

60g chilled butter

1 onion, diced

2 garlic cloves, sliced

1 celery stick, diced

½ celeriac, cut into large dice

400ml vegetable stock

2½ teaspoons matcha powder

Season the pork generously with salt and leave to one side.

For the celeriac matcha purée, melt 20g of the butter in
a saucepan over a low-medium heat and add the onion,
garlic and celery. Add a generous pinch of salt and cook
until slightly softened, about 5 minutes. Stir in the
diced celeriac and cook for a further 5 minutes, stirring
occasionally. Add the stock, cover with a lid and bring to
a simmer. When the celeriac is soft and cooked through,
add the matcha powder and simmer for another couple
of minutes.

Dice the remaining chilled butter. Use a hand-held
blender to purée the mixture, adding the diced butter one
piece at a time until a silky smooth texture is achieved.
Keep this to one side covered in baking paper to stop a
skin from forming.

Toast the hazelnuts in a dry frying pan over a low heat.
Once they are lightly browned throughout the whole nut,
coarsely crush them using a pestle and mortar.

Thinly slice the fennel, either by hand or with
a mandolin. Add to a bowl with the sherry vinegar
and olive oil and toss gently to allow the flavours
to mingle.

Place a griddle pan over a high heat. Rub the vegetable
oil over the pork and griddle until cooked through –
about 8 minutes each side depending on the size.
Season with pepper, cover with foil and leave to rest
for several minutes.

Slice the pork loin into medallions. Pool the celeriac
purée into the bottom of a shallow bowl. Lay the
medallions on top of the purée and top with the fennel
salad. Sprinkle over the crushed hazelnuts and cress.

MATCHA BURGER

Burgers get a bad wrap for being unhealthy, but when you make your own, you know exactly what you are putting in it, so you can choose good-quality, lean mince. While the Cheddar and brioche bun definitely make this a bit of treat, the burger itself is made from simple ingredients.

For the burgers

1 onion, finely chopped

1 teaspoon olive oil, plus extra
     for frying

2 teaspoons matcha powder

400g beef mince

1 egg

1 tablespoon Dijon mustard

1 tablespoon Worcestershire sauce

pinch of sea salt

For the onion jam

30g butter

220g red onion, sliced

1 tablespoon balsamic vinegar

To serve

4 slices of Cheddar cheese
     (optional)

4 brioche buns, halved and
     lightly grilled

10g unsalted butter

80g baby spinach

1 avocado, peeled, stoned
     and sliced

pea shoots or salad leaves

Sauté the onion in the teaspoon of olive oil for about 10 minutes over a low-medium heat until soft and translucent, stirring in the matcha powder after a couple of minutes.

Tip the onions along with all the other burger ingredients into a bowl and combine thoroughly with your hands. Divide into 4 patties, cover with clingfilm and place in the freezer for 10 minutes.

To make the onion jam, heat a saucepan and melt the butter. Add the onions and a splash of balsamic vinegar. Cook over a low heat for 1½ hours, until the onions are very soft and jam like.

To cook the burgers, heat a little olive oil in a griddle pan until very hot. Add 2 burgers at a time, cooking for 3–4 minutes on each side, depending on how you like your burger. When you flip the burger, add a slice of cheese, if using, to the top of the burger so that it melts.

Heat a frying pan and add 10g butter. Once melted, sauté the spinach over a high heat for a minute until wilted.

Rest the burgers for a couple of minutes before serving in the brioche buns with onion jam, spinach, avocado and pea shoots or salad leaves.

SWEETS

CREME BRULEE

This recipe is for when you really want to impress. Once you get the knack of making smooth and silky crème brûlées, it's a brilliant dessert to be able to fall back on, plus the matcha adds an extra wow factor and delicious edge to the creamy caramel.

5 egg yolks

2 teaspoons matcha powder

50g golden caster sugar, plus extra for sprinkling

450ml double cream

100ml whole milk

1 teaspoon vanilla extract

Preheat the oven to 180°C (350°F), Gas Mark 4. Place 4 ramekin dishes in a roasting tin or large cake tin. This needs to be deep enough so that you can lay an oven tray over the top without touching the top of the ramekins.

Whisk the egg yolks, matcha powder and sugar in a bowl using a hand-held electric whisk until pale and a bit fluffy.

Add the double cream, milk and vanilla extract to a pan and bring almost to the boil. As soon as bubbles appear at the edge of the pan remove from the heat.

Slowly pour the hot cream into the eggs and sugar, continuously stirring with a wire whisk as you do so. Pour this mixture through a fine sieve into another bowl and then scoop off any foam sitting on top of the liquid and discard.

Pour hot water from the tap into the roasting tin until it comes 1.5cm up the sides of the ramekins. Give the brûlée mixture a stir and pour into the ramekins until

filled right to the top. Place in the oven and top with the roasting tray so that the ramekins are covered (but not touching the tray), while leaving a little space at the edge of the roasting tin for steam to escape.

Bake for 30–35 minutes until the mixture is set but still slightly wobbly. Lift out of the roasting tin with gloves and cool on a wire rack for 2 minutes before transferring to the refrigerator for at least 4 hours or overnight.

When you are ready to serve, clean the edges of the ramekins with a piece of damp kitchen paper, sprinkle with sugar and use a blowtorch to caramelize.

MATCHA ETON MESS

For an even easier version of this, you can use pre-made meringues, but it's even more delicious when you make your own. Prepare the Eton mess on the same day while the meringues are super-fresh.

270g raspberries, washed
   and patted dry
1 teaspoon honey
250ml double cream
2 teaspoons matcha powder,
   plus extra for dusting
20g caster sugar

For the meringues
1 egg white
pinch of sea salt
230g caster sugar

Start by making the meringues. Preheat the oven to 140°C (275°F), Gas Mark 1 and line a baking tray with baking paper.

Put the egg whites into a clean bowl with the salt and whisk until they hold soft peaks. Add half the sugar and whisk to blend well with the egg white. Add the remaining sugar and whisk again until the mixture is thick and shiny and holds stiff peaks.

Dollop large spoonfuls of meringue onto the lined sheet, flattening them slightly with the back of the spoon. Bake in the oven for 2 hours until the meringues are completely dry and crisp on the outside (they will still be a bit squidgy in the middle) and can be lifted off the paper easily. Remove and leave to cool in a dry place.

Blitz 150g of the raspberries with the honey in a blender until you have a smooth sauce and set aside. Gently whisk the cream, matcha powder and sugar together until it is very lightly whipped.

Break the meringues into bite-sized pieces and fill a shallow serving platter with meringue, matcha cream, raspberry sauce and remaining whole raspberries. Decorate the tops with a dusting of matcha powder.

MATCHA LOLLIPOPS

The white chocolate is an extra treat here, but if you prefer milk or dark chocolate then go for it. Using Greek yogurt with honey means that you don't need to add any sweetener, although you can just use natural Greek yogurt and add 1–2 tablespoons of honey, according to your taste.

500g Greek yogurt with honey

2 teaspoons matcha powder

½ teaspoon vanilla extract

100g white chocolate, broken into pieces

2 teaspoons cacao nibs

2 teaspoons hazelnuts, crushed

Whisk together the Greek yogurt, matcha powder and vanilla extract until thoroughly combined.

Divide the mixture between 6 lolly moulds. Insert a wooden lolly stick into the centre of each mould and freeze for at least 6 hours.

Before serving, melt the chocolate by putting it in a heatproof bowl and setting over a saucepan of barely simmering water. Stir until melted and then set aside.

Take the lolly moulds out of the freezer and hold under the cold tap for a few seconds until you can release the lollies from the moulds. Dip into the melted chocolate or, using a spoon, drizzle the chocolate over the sides. Sprinkle over the cacao nibs and hazelnuts.

Serve as soon as the chocolate sets.

MATCHA LIME YOGURT AND CARAMELIZED PINEAPPLE

The matcha lime yogurt is such a simple recipe but it's a great idea for how to use matcha really easily in the kitchen. For a dairy-free option go for a vegan coconut yogurt. The yogurt is great on its own as a snack or with Matcha Granola (see page 32) or caramelized fruit as we've shown here, although simple fresh pineapple and berries would also work well.

For the Matcha Lime Yogurt

400g Greek yogurt

1 teaspoon matcha powder

zest and juice of ½ lime

For the pineapple

200g fresh pineapple wedges

20g unsalted butter

1 tablespoon coconut sugar

25ml sake

To serve

sprigs of mint

2 teaspoons pink peppercorns

2 teaspoons buckwheat, toasted

First make the matcha yogurt. Mix together the yogurt, matcha and lime zest and juice, adjusting to your taste.

For the pineapple, melt the butter in a heavy-based frying pan over a medium heat. Evenly sprinkle the pineapple wedges with coconut sugar and when the butter is bubbling hot, add the pineapple to the pan and griddle on each side until golden and caramelized. Add the sake and flambé for a few seconds.

Serve the hot pineapple with yogurt and fresh mint, then sprinkle with peppercorns and toasted buckwheat.

AFFOGATO

Affogato is traditionally made with espresso coffee, but this matcha version looks even more dramatic and tastes amazing. You can make it even easier and use your favourite ice cream; it will work just as well with vanilla or coconut.

500ml double cream
60g chopped stem ginger
seeds from 1 vanilla pod
3 tablespoons stem ginger syrup
200ml Classic Matcha Tea (see
    page 18)

Pour the double cream into a large bowl and use a hand-held electric mixer to whisk it until it forms stiff peaks. Add the ginger, vanilla seeds and syrup, mix well and scrape into a plastic container.

Pop into the freezer for 20 minutes, then take out and stir. Return to the freezer for another hour.

Meanwhile, make your matcha tea and pour into a lovely jug. To serve, scoop the frozen cream into glasses and pour the tea over the top.

BEAUTY

MATCHA FACE MASK

This is the perfect weekly face mask. The clay allows the pores in your skin to release impurities without drying your skin. Matcha adds a hit of antioxidants, which work hard to fight skin damaging free radicals, combatting signs of ageing. Matcha is also an effective anti-inflammatory, helping to treat skin imperfections including acne and rosacea. Unlike regular green tea, its powdered form means that matcha can easily be added to a face mask recipe.

30g bentonite clay
70ml filtered water
½ teaspoon ceremonial grade
   matcha powder

Add the clay and water to a non-metallic bowl and stir with a wooden or ceramic spoon to a thick, smooth consistency.

Add the matcha powder and continue to stir until completely combined.

To use, apply to damp skin, avoiding the eye area. Relax and leave for 5 minutes before rinsing off with warm water.

MATCHA FACE CLEANSER

Honey is a wonderful natural anti-inflammatory, while matcha is packed with antioxidants, making this a dual-action cleanser. Soapwort, which as its name implies is a natural soap, will create a slight foam, but as it is all natural ingredients you won't see lots of bubbles with this cleanser.

3 tablespoons honey
3 tablespoons avocado oil
2 tablespoons soapwort extract
½ teaspoon culinary matcha
   powder

Put all the ingredients in a small bowl and whisk together with a small whisk until thoroughly combined. Transfer to an airtight jar.

To use, wet your skin and apply a small amount of the cleanser to your face in a circular motion, avoiding the eye area. Rinse off with warm water and pat your face dry with a clean towel.

MATCHA BODY SCRUB

This is an aromatic scrub that will exfoliate the skin on your body,
leaving it soft and pampered.

---

2 teaspoons culinary matcha
  powder
50g Dead Sea salt
5 drops of lemongrass essential oil
50g coconut oil, melted
filtered water (optional)

Mix the matcha powder and salt together in a bowl, before adding the lemongrass essential oil and coconut oil and mixing thoroughly. Add a little filtered water, if needed, to achieve a typical scrub consistency and transfer to an airtight jar.

In the shower, step aside from the water flow to apply the scrub to wet skin. Massage gently into the skin gently before rinsing off.

MATCHA MAGNESIUM BATH

Magnesium flakes are wonderful for soothing muscle aches and pains. Combined with matcha, jojoba and lemon zest, this is the ultimate bath soak.

250g Epsom salts
1 tablespoon culinary matcha
    powder
2 tablespoons jojoba oil
zest of ½ lemon

Combine all the ingredients in a jar and stir well.

Add to a warm bath or foot bath, swirling into the water to dissolve the salts. Soak and enjoy for at least 20 minutes.

INDEX

◇◇◇◇◇◇